Contents

What you need to know about the National Tests

Preparing and practising for the Science Test

Instructions

Test A (Levels 4–7)	1
Test B (Levels 4–7)	25
Answers	49
Determining your level	65
Marking Grid	66

What you need to know about the National Tests

KEY STAGE 3 NATIONAL TESTS: HOW THEY WORK

Students between the ages of 11 and 14 (Years 7–9) cover Key Stage 3 of the National Curriculum. In May of their final year of Key Stage 3 (Year 9), all students take written National Tests (commonly known as SATs) in English, Mathematics and Science. The tests are carried out in school, under the supervision of teachers, but are marked by examiners outside the school.

The tests help to show what you have learned in these key subjects. They also help parents and teachers to know whether students are reaching the standards set out in the National Curriculum. The results may be used by your teacher to help place you in the appropriate teaching group for some of your GCSE courses.

Each student will probably spend around seven hours in total sitting the tests during one week in May. Most students will do two test papers in each of English, Maths and Science.

The school sends the papers away to external examiners for marking. The school will then report the results of the tests to you and your parents by the end of July, along with the results of assessments made by teachers in the classroom, based on your work throughout Key Stage 3. You will also receive a summary of the results for all students at the school, and for students nationally. This will help you to compare your performance with that of other students of the same age. The report from your school will explain to you what the results show about your progress, strengths, particular achievements and targets for development. It may also explain how to follow up the results with your teachers.

UNDERSTANDING YOUR LEVEL OF ACHIEVEMENT

The National Curriculum divides standards for performance in each subject into a number of levels, from one to eight. On average, students are expected to advance one level for every two years they are at school. By Year 9 (the end of Key Stage 3), you should be at Level 5 or 6. The table on page iii shows how you are expected to progress through the levels at ages 7, 11 and 14 (the end of Key Stages 1, 2 and 3).

There are different National Test papers for different ability levels. This is to ensure that you can show positive achievement on the test, and not be discouraged by trying to answer questions which are too easy or too difficult. For Science, the tests are grouped into two ranges of levels, called 'tiers'. The two tiers cover Levels 3–6 and Levels 5–7. Your teachers will decide which tier you should be entered for. Each tier has two test papers. Each paper will be one hour long. Extension papers with high level questions are also available for exceptionally able students.

What you need to know about the National Tests

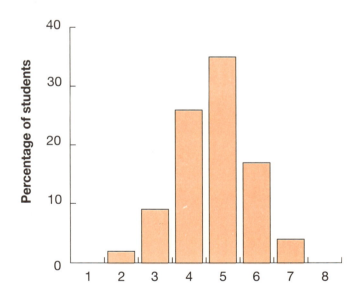

How you should progress

This book concentrates on Levels 4–7. This means that you will find plenty of questions to practise, regardless of which tier you are entered for. The bar chart below shows you what percentage of students nationally reached each of the levels in the 1996 tests for Science.

Levels achieved in Science, 1996

Preparing and practising for the Science Test

SCIENCE AT KEY STAGE 3
The questions in this book will test you on the Key Stage 3 curriculum for Science. For assessment purposes, the National Curriculum divides Science into four sections, called Attainment Targets (ATs). The first AT, Scientific Investigation, is assessed only by the teacher in the classroom, not in the written tests. The other three ATs are:

- AT2: Life Processes and Living Things (which is largely Biology)
- AT3: Materials and their Properties (which is largely Chemistry)
- AT4: Physical Processes (which is largely Physics)

The National Curriculum describes levels of performance for each of the four Science ATs. These AT levels are taken together to give an overall level for Science. The test papers have questions covering each of ATs 2–4.

USING THIS BOOK TO HELP YOU PREPARE
This book contains four basic features:

Questions:	two test papers for Levels 4–7
Answers:	showing acceptable responses and marks
Examiner's Tips:	giving advice on how to avoid common mistakes and improve your score
Level Charts:	showing you how to interpret your marks to arrive at a level for each test, as well as an overall level

SETTING THE TESTS AT HOME
Take Test A first. Mark the test to see how you have done, working through the answers and advice given. Then take Test B on a different day. You should carry out the tests in a place where you are comfortable. You will need a pencil, a rubber and a ruler. Make sure to read the instructions on page vi carefully before you begin.

Note the starting time in the box at the top of each test. Time yourself during the test, using a clock, a watch, or the help of a parent or friend. During the test, if you do not understand a word, you can ask a parent or other adult to explain what the word means, providing it is not a scientific word. For example, you could ask someone to explain what is meant by the word 'function' but not 'evaporation' or 'pressure'.

After 60 minutes, stop writing. If you have not finished, but wish to continue working on the test, draw a line to show how much has been completed within the test time. Then continue for as long as you wish.

Preparing and practising for the Science Test

MARKING THE QUESTIONS
When you have completed a test, turn to the Answers section at the back of the book. Work through the answers, using the advice in the Examiner's Tips to correct mistakes and explain problems. If you required extra time to complete a test, go through all the answers, but do not include the marks for the 'extra' questions in the total scores.

Using the recommended answers, award yourself the appropriate mark or marks for each question. In the margin of each test page, there are small boxes divided in half. The marks available for each question are at the bottom; write your score in the top half of the box.

Enter the total number of marks for each question on the Marking Grid on page 66. Then add them up to find the total for the test. Look at the Level Charts on page 65 to determine your level for each test, as well as an overall level.

FINALLY, AS THE TESTS DRAW NEAR
In the days before the tests, make sure you are as relaxed and confident as possible. You can help yourself by:

- ensuring you know what test papers you will be doing;

- working through practice questions, and learning which answers are right and why.

Above all, don't worry too much! Although the National Tests are important, your achievement throughout the school year is equally important. Do your best in these tests; that is all anyone can ask.

Instructions

Each test should take 60 minutes.

Try to answer all the questions.

Read the questions carefully. Sometimes you will use your knowledge to answer the questions. Other times the question will give you a situation you have not met before. When this is the case, you will be given all the information you need to answer the question.

If you think, after reading a question carefully, that you cannot answer it, leave the question and come back to it later.

The questions you have to answer are given in orange boxes. For example,

> **What is happening to the speed of the yacht? Explain how you can tell.**

Write your answers fully on the test papers in this book. The ✏️➤ shows where you should answer the question. The lines or space given should give you some indication of what is expected.

Look at the number of marks for each part of a question. This is shown in the box in the margin, for example,

2

If a question is worth one mark, often a single word or single point is needed. A question worth two marks would need two distinct points to be made. You are very unlikely to score two marks with a single word answer.

Look carefully at the words you write, particularly scientific words. Read your answers carefully to yourself and make sure you have clearly expressed what you mean.

GOOD LUCK!

Test A

Start ☐ **Finish** ☐

1 The diagram shows the parts of a flower mounted on a piece of paper.

a Use words from the list below to fill in the missing labels.

anther   ovary   sepal   stamen   style

- stigma
- (i) ....
- (ii) ....
- (iii) ....
- petals
- (iv) ....

b What is the job of each of the following parts of the flower?

(i) sepals ....

(ii) anther ....

(iii) petals ....

c Explain the difference between **pollination** and **fertilisation**.

(i) pollination ....

....

(ii) fertilisation ....

....

d The diagram shows a bumble bee inside a foxglove flower.

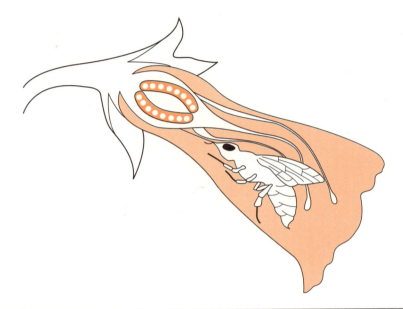

(i) What substance is the bumble bee taking from the flower?

....

(ii) What does the bumble bee use this substance for?

....

(iii) Pollen is removed from the flower on to the bumble bee's back.

How does the structure of this flower help the bumble bee to pick up pollen?

....

....

(iv) The large open flower hangs down at a slight angle.

Suggest why it does this.

....

e The diagram shows a grass flower. Grass flowers are not very noticeable as they have no petals.

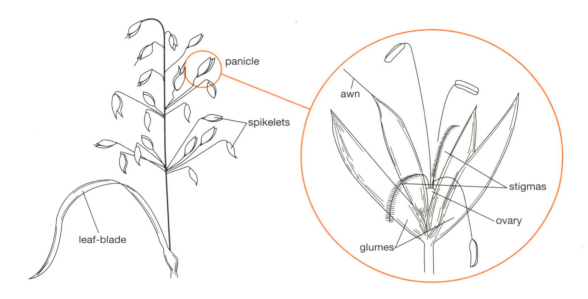

These flowers are pollinated by the wind.

Explain how each of the following features increases the chance that grass flowers will be pollinated.

(i) The flowers are on slender stalks.

....

....

(ii) The stigmas are feathery and outside the flower.

....

2 The diagram shows a system of organs in humans.

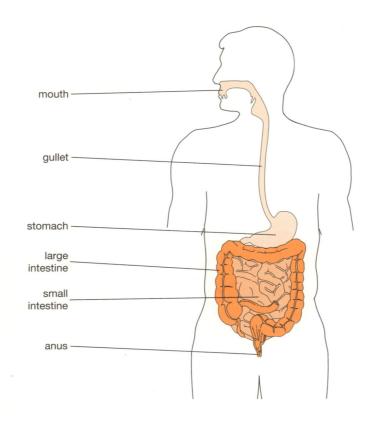

a Underline the organ system shown in the diagram.

 breathing   digestive   nervous   reproductive   skeletal

Test A

b Match each named organ with its job. Draw lines to link each organ to the job it does. One has been done for you.

Organ	Job
mouth	absorbs dissolved food into the blood
gullet	chews the food into small pieces
stomach	passes solid waste out of the body
large intestine	passes the food to the stomach
small intestine	dissolves the food
anus	absorbs water from the waste

c Saliva in the mouth contains an enzyme that changes starch into sugar so that the food can be absorbed into the blood.

Explain why sugar can be absorbed into the blood but starch cannot.

....

....

3 This question is about **temporary** and **permanent** changes.

A **temporary** change is one which can be reversed easily, either by cooling or by mixing the substances produced. If ice is heated it turns to liquid water. If the water is cooled, ice is reformed.

A **permanent** change is one which cannot be reversed, either by cooling or by mixing the products. Once it has taken place it cannot be reversed. Burning a piece of wood is a permanent change.

The table below gives information about the heating of seven substances.

	Appearance before heating	Change on heating	Change on cooling	Change in mass of test tube and contents
Cobalt chloride crystals	purple crystals	pale blue powder (water, steam)	pale blue powder	decreased
Zinc oxide	white solid	yellow solid	white solid	unchanged
Potassium manganate(VII) crystals	purple crystals	colourless gas, fine black solid, dark green solid	black solid, dark green solid	decreased
Silicon dioxide	white solid	white solid	white solid	unchanged
Sulphur	yellow solid	brown liquid	yellow solid	unchanged
Ammonium chloride	white solid	colourless gas	white solid formed	unchanged
Copper		glows red	black	increased

Test A

a Write down the names of **FOUR** substances which undergo temporary changes on heating.

....

....

b Write down the names of **TWO** substances which undergo permanent changes on heating.

....

....

4 Red cabbage can be used as an indicator to detect acids and alkalis.

Here are the instructions on how to make the indicator, but they are in the wrong order.

A Filter the mixture.

B Add 25 cm^3 of ethanol.

C Leave to cool.

D Cut up some leaves into small pieces.

E Heat up the mixture in a water bath.

a Put the letters of the instructions in the correct order.

D → ☐ → ☐ → ☐ → A

b Draw a diagram of the apparatus which could be used to separate the bits of red cabbage from the indicator solution.

c This indicator was added to solutions of different pH. The results are shown in the table.

pH of solution	1	5	7	9	11
colour of red cabbage indicator	red	red	red	green	green

Complete the following sentences.

In acid solutions the red cabbage indicator will be .... in colour.

In neutral solutions the red cabbage indicator will be .... in colour.

In alkaline solutions the red cabbage indicator will be .... in colour.

d Which of the following substances could turn the red colour of the red cabbage indicator to green? Underline the correct answer.

hydrochloric acid   vinegar   washing powder   water

e The table shows the colour changes of four different indicators at different pH values.

	pH				
	1 2 3	4 5 6	7 8 9	10 11	12 13 14
	strong acid	weak acid	neutral	weak alkali	strong alkali
Universal Indicator	red	orange	green	blue	purple
red litmus	red	red	blue	blue	blue
blue litmus	red	red	blue	blue	blue
methyl orange	red	orange	orange	orange	orange

(i) Describe how red litmus paper and blue litmus paper can be used to show that a solution is neutral.

(ii) Explain why a mixture of equal volumes of Universal Indicator and methyl orange will turn brown when added to a neutral solution.

5 The diagrams show a plant cell and an animal cell.

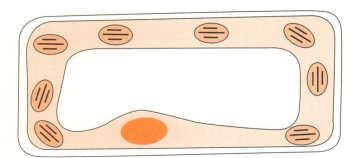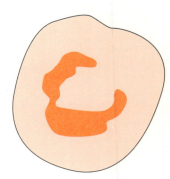

Write down THREE things which are in the plant cell but not in the animal cell.

(i) ....

(ii) ....

(iii) ....

6 Body cells obtain energy by respiration.

Use words from the list to complete the following paragraph about respiration.

| blood | glucose | heart | kidneys | liver | lungs | oxygen |

The two important substances used in respiration are ....

and .... These are taken to all parts of the body by the

.... The waste products of respiration are carbon

dioxide and water. Carbon dioxide is excreted in the ....

and water is removed from the blood by the ....

7 The table contains information about five elements labelled **A–E**.

	State at room temperature	Dull or shiny	Colour	Electrical conductivity	Magnetic
A	solid	dull	yellow	nil	no
B	solid	dull	grey	good	yes
C	liquid	shiny	silver	good	no
D	solid	dull	red	nil	no
E	solid	dull	grey	good	no

a Which of the elements A–E are metals?

....

b Which of the elements could be iron?

....

8 Manganese is a metallic element. The bar chart shows its melting point and boiling point.

Thallium is another metal with a melting point of 300 °C and a boiling point of 1450 °C.

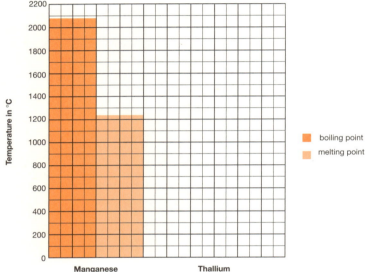

a Complete the bar chart by putting in the melting point and boiling point of thallium.

b Write down the melting point and boiling point of manganese.

Melting point .... °C   Boiling point .... °C

c Circle the temperature at which both manganese and thallium are in the same state.

400 °C   1000 °C   1400 °C   2000 °C

d Describe a test which could be used to show that manganese and thallium are metals. You should draw a diagram and give the result of the test.

Result: ....

9 Five groups of students carried out an experiment, burning different masses of magnesium ribbon in air to form magnesium oxide.

The apparatus they used is shown in the diagram below.

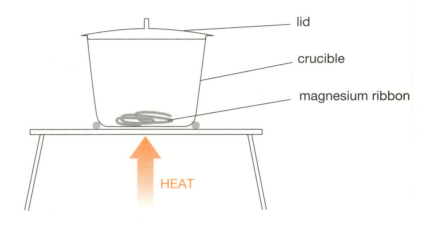

Their results are shown in the table.

	A	B	C	D	E
Mass of magnesium in g	0.9	1.2	1.5	1.8	2.1
Mass of magnesium oxide formed in g	1.5	2.0	2.5	2.7	3.5
Mass of oxygen in g	0.6				

a Finish the table by working out the mass of oxygen combined in each experiment. One has been done for you.

b On the grid opposite plot the results of each group. The results for group **A** have been done for you. Draw the best straight line through the points.

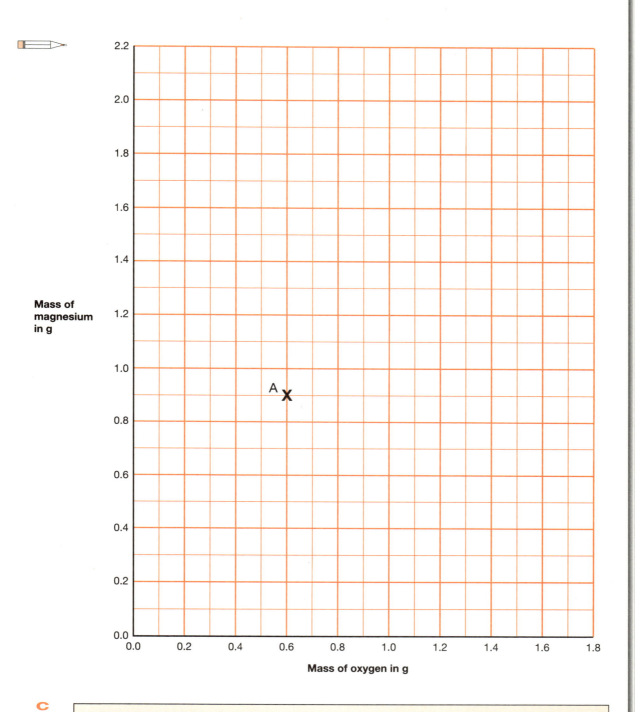

c From the graph, why do you think that the results of group **D** are not correct?

....

d During the experiment the students were told to lift the crucible lid from time to time.

(i) Why is it important to lift the crucible lid during the experiment?

....

(ii) At the end of the experiment what do you think remained in the crucible of group D, apart from magnesium oxide?

....

10 The table contains the properties of five substances labelled **V–Z**.

	Melting point in °C	Boiling point in °C	Electrical conductivity when solid	Electrical conductivity when melted	Effect of heating in air
V	800	1470	none	good	no reaction
W	98	880	good	good	burns to form a solid oxide
X	–30	58	none	none	burns to form carbon dioxide and steam
Y	114	444	none	none	burns to form a gaseous oxide
Z	1700	2200	none	none	no reaction

a Which substance is a metal?

  ....

b Which two substances are compounds?

  .... and ....

Q10a

Q10b

11 Two balloons are given the same type of charge by rubbing them with a duster. They are then hung near to each other using pieces of string fixed to the ceiling.

a **Which diagram shows the positions of the charged balloons correctly?**

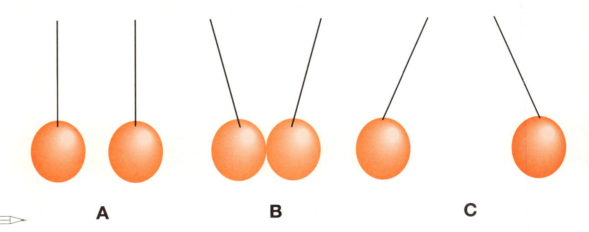

A   B   C

Underline the letter of your choice.

b The charged balloons have a negative charge. When the duster is held near one of the balloons, the balloon moves towards the duster.

What type of charge does the duster have?

c **Explain how rubbing the balloon with the duster causes both things to become charged.**

12 Three circuits are shown in the diagram.

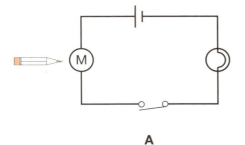 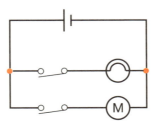 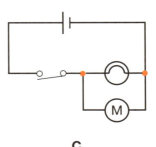

A   **B**   **C**

a Which circuit allows the motor to be on when the lamp is off?

....

b Draw an **A** on diagram C to show where you could put an ammeter to measure the current **in the motor** when the circuit is switched on.

c The next circuit shows three ammeters being used to measure the current entering and leaving two lamps in series.

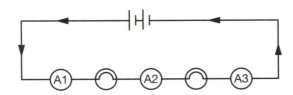

The reading on ammeter A1 is 2.0 A. Write down the readings on ammeters A2 and A3.

(i) A2 reads ....

(ii) A3 reads ....

13 The table shows the times taken for the runners to finish a 75 metre race.

Runner	Time/s
Claire	12
Paul	15
David	13
Laura	14
John	10

a Who won the race?

....

b Who was the slowest runner?

....

c Work out Paul's speed in m/s.

speed = ... m/s

14 A drawing pin has a sharp point and a flat head.

a Explain why drawing pins can pierce things easily.

....

....

b A tank weighs 75 000 N and the area of the caterpillar tracks touching the ground is 15 m².

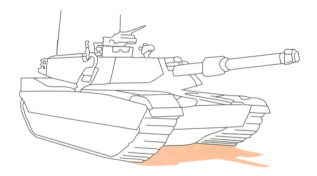

Work out the pressure it causes on the ground.

pressure = ...

15 Some things give out light and other things reflect light.

a Underline the objects that give out light.

candle flame   cat's eye   the Moon   the Sun   television screen

b In a theatre, very bright lights shine on to the stage.

Explain how the audience is able to see the actors and the stage.

....

....

c The bright lights used to light up a stage are often fitted with colour filters.

Underline the colours that would pass through a yellow filter unchanged.

blue   green   magenta   red   turquoise   yellow

d An actor wearing a blue costume has yellow light shining on him.

What colour does his costume look to be?

....

16 The diagrams show the position of the Sun in the sky at midday in spring and in summer.

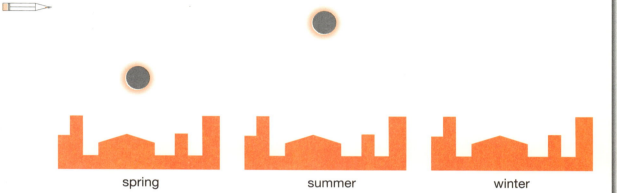

spring   summer   winter

a Draw the position of the Sun in winter.

b What causes the Sun's position in the sky to change?

....

c Venus is easily seen as a bright yellow planet in the sky. Uranus can only be seen with a telescope.

Write down **TWO** reasons why Venus appears much brighter than Uranus.

....

....

17a Underline the energy resources in the list that are renewable.

biomass   coal   oil   wind

b Explain why wood is classified as a renewable energy resource.

....

18 Electrical appliances transfer energy from the electricity supply.

a Complete the energy flow diagram for an electric fan heater.

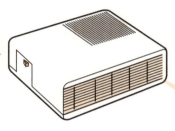

energy from electricity

energy as ....
and ....

b Complete the diagram to show the energy flow through a lamp in one second.

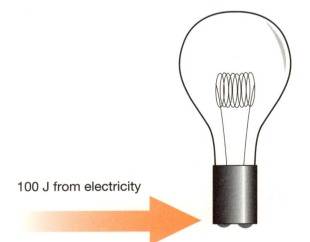

4 J light

100 J from electricity

Test B

Start ☐ Finish ☐

1 Here is a simple food chain.

Cabbage leaves ⟶ caterpillars ⟶ great tit ⟶ sparrowhawk

a Which item in this food chain is a herbivore?

....

b Why must a food chain always start with a plant?

....

c What do the arrows in this food chain show?

....

d Explain how the great tit is both <u>predator</u> and <u>prey</u>.

(i) predator ....

(ii) prey ....

Here is a food web.

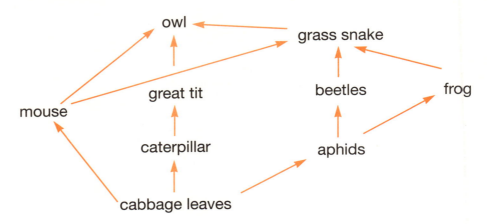

e   **The owl is a tertiary consumer. Write down the name of another tertiary consumer.**

    ....

f   The number of great tits would fall if there was a shortage of caterpillars. The number of grass snakes would not be reduced in the same way if there was a shortage of beetles.

    Explain why.

    ....
    ....

2 The diagram shows part of the inside of the human body.

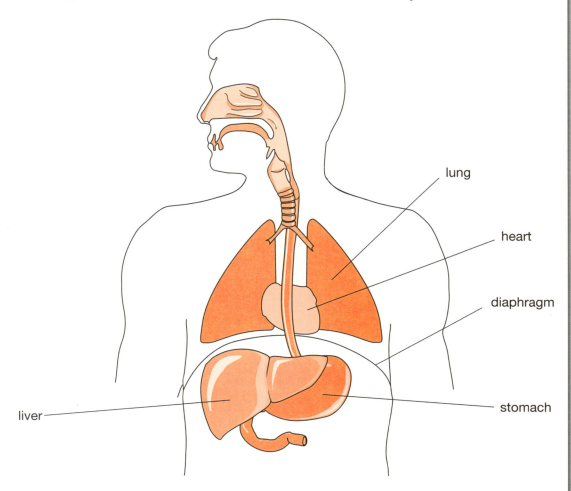

Finish the table below by choosing the correct organ from the list which carries out each job shown in the table.

Job of the organ	Name of the organ
Pumps blood around the body	
Exchanges gases between air and blood	
Processes nitrogen waste (urea)	
Digests food	

3 The diagram shows part of an arm.

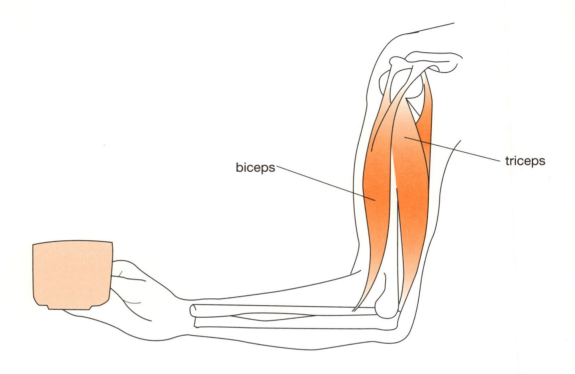

a What type of joint is the elbow?

....

b Explain how the muscles raise the forearm when a person drinks from a cup.

....

c How is the arm lowered again?

....

4   The diagrams show the steps which should be taken to produce new plants by taking cuttings using hormone rooting powder.

A Remove most of the leaves   B Cut off a sideshoot   C Put it in compost   D Dip it in rooting compound

a   The diagrams are in the wrong order.

Fill in the boxes to show the correct order.

☐ → ☐ → ☐ → ☐

b   **Why is the tip of a sideshoot better than a piece of older stem when taking cuttings?**

....

c   **Suggest TWO reasons why most, but not all, of the leaves are removed from the cutting.**

....

....

Q4a — 3

Q4b — 1

Q4c — 2

5a The diagram shows a xylem cell taken from the stem of a plant.

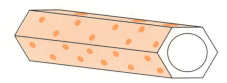

(i) What is the job of the xylem cell in the plant?

....

(ii) How does the structure of the xylem cell make it suitable for this?

....

....

b Leaves can be regarded as the 'factories' of the plant. In sunlight, photosynthesis takes place in green leaves. Carbon dioxide and water are converted into sugar in the presence of the green substance called chlorophyll. Oxygen gas is also produced.

(i) Finish the word equation for photosynthesis.

.... + ... + energy

⟶ .... + ...

(ii) A variegated ivy plant has leaves which are green and yellow.

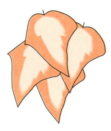

Why does this plant produce less sugar than a green ivy?

....

c The graph below shows how much sugar is produced by a green ivy plant over a period of several days when kept in a greenhouse.

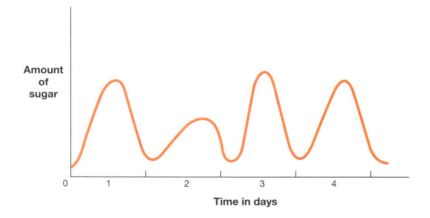

(i) Suggest one reason why less sugar might have been produced during day 2.

....

(ii) Draw a line on the graph to show how much sugar would be produced if the plant was kept under bright light all the time.

d Photosynthesis does not take place in a plant which is kept in the dark.

(i) What process takes place in a plant in both the light and the dark?

....

(ii) What gas do plants absorb from the air at night?

....

6 The diagram shows an ice lolly, a car tyre and a thermometer. The small diagrams show the arrangement of particles in each of them.

a An ice lolly is solid.

(i) Why does an ice lolly keep its shape?

....

(ii) What happens to the ice lolly when it gets warmer?

....

(iii) What happens to the particles in the ice lolly when it gets warmer?

....

b A car tyre contains a gas.

> What property of a gas makes it suitable for filling a car tyre?

....

c > Which of the following properties of a liquid makes it suitable for use in a thermometer? Underline your answer.

      Can be poured

      Heavy

      Expands on heating

      Can run your hand through it

d The diagram shows how a liquid can be used in a car braking system.

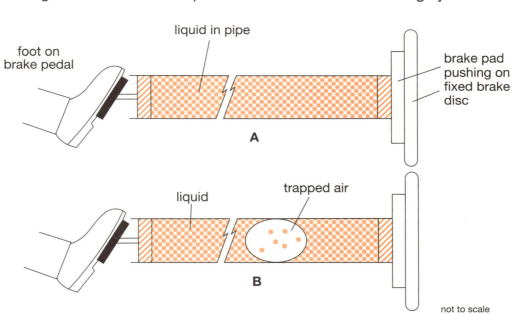

> Explain why the trapped air in diagram **B** stops the brake from working.

....

....

33

7 The diagrams show three methods which can be used to separate mixtures of substances.

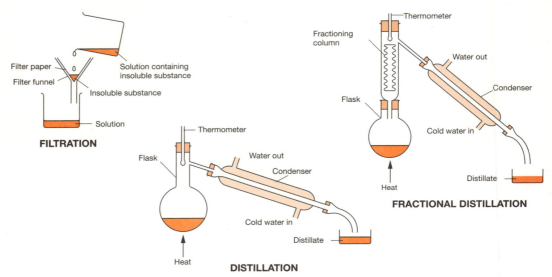

The table contains information about three substances labelled **P**, **Q** and **R**.

Substance	State at room temperature	Solubility in water	Boiling point in °C
P	solid	soluble	above 1000
Q	liquid	soluble	80
R	solid	insoluble	above 1000

Which of the three methods would be best to separate each of the following mixtures?

a Water from a mixture of **P** and water

....

b **R** from a mixture of **P**, **Q**, **R** and water

....

c **Q** from a mixture of **Q** and water

....

8 Experiments were carried out with four metals and dilute hydrochloric acid. The metals were copper, iron, magnesium and zinc. The diagrams show the results obtained when pieces of the four metals were added to dilute hydrochloric acid. Three of the test tubes were then heated and the results are also shown.

Without heating

copper   iron   magnesium   zinc

On heating

copper   iron   zinc

a **Use the results of these reactions to arrange the four metals in order of reactivity.**

.... most reactive

....

....

.... least reactive

b **Finish the word equation for the reaction of magnesium and hydrochloric acid.**

magnesium
+   ⟶   .... + ...
hydrochloric acid

9 Zinc and sulphur are elements. When they are mixed together and the mixture is heated, a reaction takes place.

a Name the compound formed when zinc and sulphur combine together.

....

b In the diagram below:

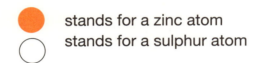

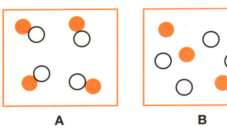 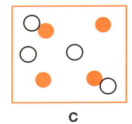 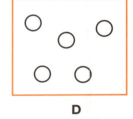

Which diagram represents each of the following?

(i) A pure element ....

(ii) A mixture of zinc and sulphur..

(iii) A compound of zinc and sulphur..

10 The diagram shows the particles of water in a liquid.

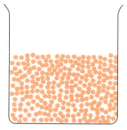

a Describe the movement of particles in liquid water.

....

....

2 Q10a

b When the beaker is left on a window sill, the water in the beaker disappears.

(i) Name the process that causes the water to disappear.

....

1 Q10b (i)

(ii) Explain what is happening to the particles in the water when the water disappears.

....

....

....

2 Q10b (ii)

(iii) When a drop of a liquid such as ethanol is placed on the back of the hand, the hand feels cold.

Explain why this is the case.

....

....

2
Q10b (iii)

c   In warm countries water reservoirs may be covered with a thin layer of oil.

Why is this done?

....

1
Q10c

11 Tests were carried out by putting four metals into four different metal nitrate solutions.

A tick ✔ means that the metal reacted with the solution and a cross ✘ means there was no reaction.

	Copper nitrate	Lead nitrate	Magnesium nitrate	Silver nitrate
Copper	✘	✘	✘	✔
Lead	✔	✘	✘	✔
Magnesium	✔	✔	✘	✔
Silver	✘	✘	✘	✘

Test B

a   **Arrange these four metals in order of reactivity.**

✏️ .... most reactive

....

....

.... least reactive

b   Copper nitrate solution is blue in colour.

What would be seen when lead is added to copper nitrate solution?

✏️ ....

....

c   When zinc is added to copper sulphate solution a reaction takes place.

Finish the word equation.

✏️   zinc   ....

  +   ⟶   +

copper sulphate   ....

12a Which diagram shows the magnetic field pattern of a bar magnet? Underline the letter of your choice.

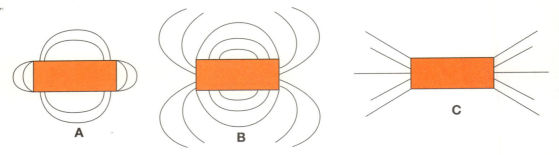

b Which diagram shows a pair of magnets that attract each other? Underline the letter of your choice.

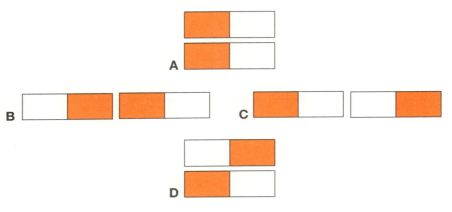

c The diagram shows the magnetic field pattern near one end of a magnetised steel bar.

The circle represents a small compass placed near the steel bar.

Draw an arrow inside the circle to show which way the north-seeking pole of the compass points.

13 The diagram shows an electromagnet made by passing a current in a coil of wire. The electromagnet is not strong enough to pick up a paperclip.

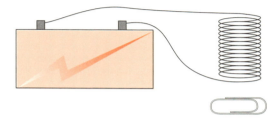

In the next diagram an iron core has been placed inside the coil.

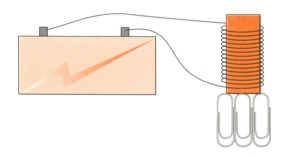

a **Explain why the electromagnet is now stronger.**

....

....

b **Write down ONE other way of making the electromagnet stronger.**

....

14 The diagram shows three different circuits.

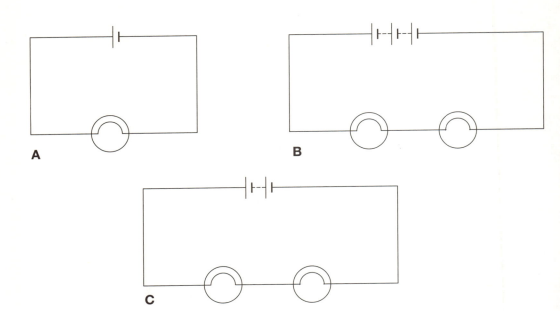

a **In which TWO circuits would the lamps be equally bright?**

....

b **In which circuit is the current greatest?**

....

15 The diagram shows a boat floating on water. The arrow represents the push of the water on the boat.

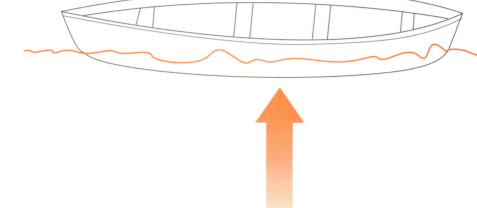

a Draw and label an arrow to show the other force acting on the boat.

b What can you tell about the sizes of the two forces acting on the boat?

....

c What happens to the upward force when a person gets into the boat?

....

16 Yachts rely on wind to push them along. The diagram shows the driving force on a yacht and the resistive force of the water.

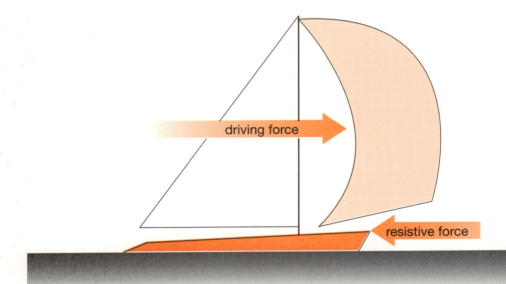

a What is happening to the speed of the yacht? Explain how you can tell.

....

....

b Explain what happens to the speed of the yacht when the wind stops blowing.

....

....

17a Which diagram shows the way in which light is reflected by a mirror? Underline your choice.

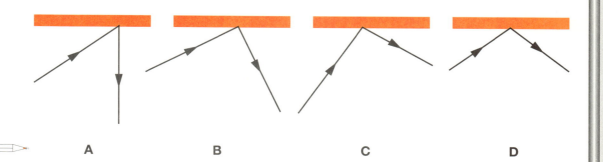

A   B   C   D

b The circle represents a boy looking at his image in a mirror.

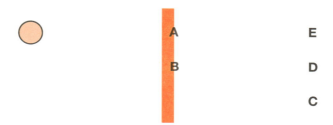

(i) Which letter shows the position of his image?

....

(ii) Underline **THREE** words or phrases from the list that describe his image.

larger   real   same size   smaller   upright   upside down   virtual

c When light passes from air into the glass of the mirror there is a change of speed which may cause a change in direction.

Underline the word that describes this change.

diffraction   dispersion   dissipation   refraction   scattering

18 When a loudspeaker makes a sound a paper cone vibrates.

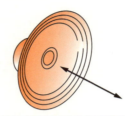

a How does the movement of the paper cone change when the loudspeaker makes a louder sound?

....

b How does the sound change when the frequency of the vibration increases?

....

19 The diagram shows the Sun's position just after sunrise on a day in **spring**.

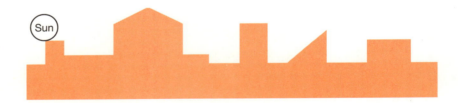

a Draw a line on the diagram to show the path of the Sun until it sets.

b Why does the Sun appear to move across the sky in this way?

....

20 The diagram shows a communications satellite in an elliptical orbit around the Earth.

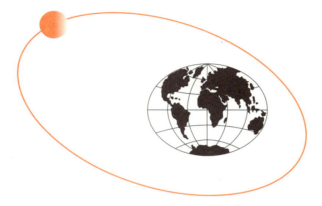

a Explain how the satellite allows links between portable telephones in Britain and those in other European countries.

....

....

2 Q20a

b Describe the force acting on the satellite in orbit.

....

....

2 Q20b

21 The diagram shows a hydro-electricity generator. At night, electricity is used to pump water from a low reservoir to a high reservoir.

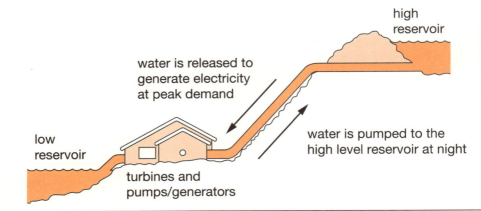

a **Describe the energy transfer that takes place when the water is used to generate electricity.**

....

....

b **Explain why the energy produced by the generator is less than the energy lost by the water.**

....

....

c **Write down TWO benefits of using this system.**

(i) ....

(ii) ....

Answers

HOW TO MARK THE QUESTIONS

When marking your tests remember the answers given are sample answers and you must look at your answers and judge whether they deserve credit. Award the mark if the answer deserves credit.

You should pay special attention to spelling. There is no automatic penalty for a word that is misspelt. Look at the word as written and read it aloud. If it sounds correct and has the correct number of syllables, the mark can be awarded. For example, 'desolve' and 'weit' are acceptable for 'dissolve' and 'weight'. However, 'photosis' would not be accepted for 'photosynthesis'.

There is an emphasis on the correct spelling of scientific words. Look through this book and make a list of correctly spelt scientific words. Looking at this list and making sure you know the meaning of the words is good preparation in the few days before the tests.

When you go through the answers, try to work out where you have gone wrong. Make a note of the key points, so that you will remember them next time.

Enter your marks for each test on the Marking Grid on page 66, and then work out your level of achievement on these tests on page 65.

TEST A — Pages 1–24

1a   Words from the top:
  (i)   ovary — 1 mark
  (ii) anther — 1 mark
  (iii) stamen — 1 mark
  (iv) sepal — 1 mark
 b (i)   Protect the flower bud — 1 mark
  (ii) Produces the pollen (which contains the male sex cells) — 1 mark
  (iii) Provide colour and scent to attract insects to the flower — 1 mark

Examiner's tip

The structure of the flower and the jobs of the main parts of a flower are commonly tested at KS3.

 c (i)   Pollination is the transfer of pollen from the stamen (or anther) to the stigma. — 1 mark
  (ii) Fertilisation is the fusion of the male and female sex cells. — 1 mark

Examiner's tip

It is important to distinguish between pollination and fertilisation. Students are often confused and use the two terms to mean the same thing. If the transfer of pollen occurs within the same flower, it is called self-pollination. If the pollen from one flower is transferred to the stigma of another flower, it is called cross-pollination. After a pollen grain has landed on a stigma, it begins to grow a pollen tube. The pollen tube grows down the style and into the ovary. Inside the ovary the nucleus from the pollen grain (male sex cell) fuses with the nucleus of the egg cell (female sex cell) and the process of fertilisation occurs.

Test A Answers

d	(i)	Nectar	1 mark
	(ii)	The bee uses the nectar for energy (to make honey).	1 mark
	(iii)	The bee has to brush against the anthers to get the nectar.	1 mark
	(iv)	To prevent rain from entering the flower.	1 mark
e	(i)	The stalks are more easily blown about in the wind so the pollen can be shaken off the flowers.	1 mark
	(ii)	There is a larger surface area to pick up passing pollen and pollen can get to the stigmas more easily when they are outside the flower.	1 mark

Examiner's tip

There are two points here and either point is sufficient for the awarding of the single mark.

TOTAL 15 MARKS

2a Digestive — 1 mark

b *The answer is shown below. Allow one mark for each correct link.*

Organ	Job
mouth	absorbs dissolved food into the blood
gullet	chews the food into small pieces
stomach	passes solid waste out of the body
large intestine	passes the food to the stomach
small intestine	dissolves the food
anus	absorbs water from the waste

5 marks

Examiner's tip

The job of the intestines is often misunderstood. The food leaves the stomach in a liquid form. It first passes through the small intestine where soluble substances pass into the blood. It then goes to the large intestine which absorbs the water, leaving solid waste which is passed out at the anus.

c Starch molecules are too large to diffuse into the blood capillaries. — 1 mark
Sugar molecules are smaller and can pass into the capillaries. — 1 mark

Examiner's tip

The enzyme works by 'chopping up' the large starch molecules into smaller molecules of sugar.

TOTAL 8 MARKS

Test A Answers

3a Cobalt chloride crystals, zinc oxide, sulphur, ammonium chloride *2 marks*
Award two marks if four are correct and only one mark if two or three are correct.

Examiner's tip
It is important to realise the difference between permanent and temporary changes. Silicon dioxide is unchanged on heating. Sulphur and ammonium chloride reform on cooling. Cobalt chloride turns back to purple on mixing the blue powder produced and water.

b Potassium manganate(VII) crystals, copper *1 mark*
Both substances are required for one mark.

TOTAL 3 MARKS

4a B E C *3 marks*
*Award three marks if the order is exactly correct. Score one mark if **B** is before **E**, one mark if **B** is before **C** and one mark if **E** is before **C**.*

Examiner's tip
This is an example of a question which tests whether you can put a series of events into the correct order. When you have completed your answer check through the order of events again to see that it is sensible.

b
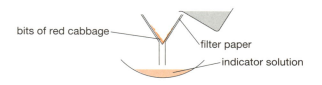
1 mark

Examiner's tip
This is a diagram showing filtration. The mark is not for the term filtration but for a diagram.

c Red, red, green *2 marks*
Award two marks if all three are correct and one mark if two are correct.

d Washing powder *1 mark*

Examiner's tip
Washing powder is the only alkali.

e (i) In a neutral solution, red litmus paper stays red. *1 mark*
In a neutral solution, blue litmus paper stays blue. *1 mark*

Test A Answers

> **Examiner's tip**
>
> Students are often very confused about the use of litmus and Universal Indicator. Litmus only shows whether a substance is acidic or alkaline by turning red or blue. Universal Indicator can turn a range of colours showing the strength of acid or alkali.

(ii) A neutral solution turns Universal Indicator green and turns methyl orange indicator orange.
A mixture of green and orange appears brown. *1 mark*

TOTAL 10 MARKS

5 (i) Cell wall — *1 mark*
  (ii) Chloroplasts — *1 mark*
  (iii) Vacuole — *1 mark*

TOTAL 3 MARKS

6 glucose and oxygen — *One mark each, either way round: 2 marks*
   blood — *1 mark*
   lungs — *1 mark*
   kidneys — *1 mark*

TOTAL 5 MARKS

7 a **B, C** and **E** — *All required: 1 mark*
  b **B** — *1 mark*

> **Examiner's tip**
>
> Here you are expected to know that metals conduct electricity and iron is magnetic.

TOTAL 2 MARKS

8 a 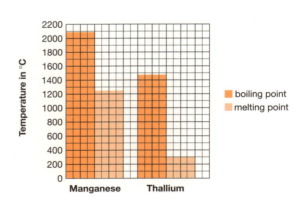 *1 mark*

  b Melting point: between 1220 °C and 1240 °C — *1 mark*
     Boiling point: between 2060 °C and 2080 °C — *1 mark*

Test A Answers

> **Examiner's tip**
>
> The answer should be within the range given in each case. Make sure that the melting point and the boiling point are the right way round – the melting point is always lower.

c   1400 °C   *1 mark*

> **Examiner's tip**
>
> Both elements are liquid at 1400°C.

d

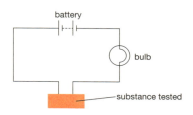

Both manganese and thallium conduct electricity so the bulb will light in each case.   *1 mark*   *1 mark*

TOTAL 6 MARKS

9a   0.8 g, 1.0 g, 0.9 g, 1.4 g   *2 marks*
All correct: two marks; two or three correct: one mark

b   Plotting   *1 mark*
Straight line drawn   *1 mark*

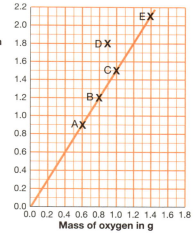

> **Examiner's tip**
>
> The straight line should pass through the origin (0,0). One point is not on the straight line. Do not be surprised if all the points do not fall on the straight line. This frequently happens with experimental results.

53

c	The point **D** is not on the straight line.	1 mark
d (i)	To let air into the crucible so that the magnesium can burn	1 mark
(ii)	Magnesium	1 mark

> **Examiner's tip**
>
> When carrying out the experiment, it is important to lift the lid to let air (oxygen) in but it is also important not to let smoke escape as this is magnesium oxide. In the case of group **D** it is likely that not all the magnesium has burned.

TOTAL 7 MARKS

10a	W	1 mark
b	**X** and **V**	Both required: 1 mark

> **Examiner's tip**
>
> This question requires understanding of elements, mixtures and compounds. When a compound burns it forms more than one product.

TOTAL 2 MARKS

11a	C	1 mark

> **Examiner's tip**
>
> You should remember that things with the same type of charge repel each other, and those with opposite types of charge attract each other.

b	Positive	1 mark
c	Negatively charged electrons	1 mark
	Move from the duster to the balloon	1 mark

> **Examiner's tip**
>
> There is one mark here for knowing that the charge is transferred between the balloon and the duster, and one mark for knowing that the charges are negative.

TOTAL 4 MARKS

12a	B	1 mark

> **Examiner's tip**
>
> In circuits **A** and **C**, when the switch is operated, the current passes in **both** the lamp and the motor.

Test A Answers

b Your **A** should be placed anywhere between the motor and one of the orange blobs. *1 mark*

Examiner's tip
It does not matter whether the ammeter is placed on the left or right side of the motor. Motors do not use up current, so the same current that passes into the motor also passes out. An ammeter placed in the top rectangle of the circuit measures the total current, i.e. the current in the motor plus the current in the lamp.

c (i) A2 reads 2.0 A *1 mark*
(ii) A3 reads 2.0 A *1 mark*

Examiner's tip
This question is testing whether you know that lamps and other circuit components do not use up any current.

TOTAL 4 MARKS

13a John *1 mark*

Examiner's tip
John won because he completed the race in the shortest time.

b Paul *1 mark*

Examiner's tip
It took Paul longer than the others to travel the same distance.

c speed = distance ÷ time *1 mark*
    = 75m ÷ 15 s = 5 m/s *1 mark*

Examiner's tip
When doing calculations you should always write out the formula first. This way, you get a mark for knowing the formula even if you make a mistake when working out the answer.

TOTAL 4 MARKS

14a The force pushes onto a small area. *1 mark*
This causes a large pressure. *1 mark*

55

Test A Answers

> **Examiner's tip**
>
> When answering questions about pressure, try to make precise statements about force and area. Avoid answers such as 'it concentrates the force'.

b   pressure = force ÷ area   1 mark
       = 75000 N ÷ 15 m^2 = 5000 N/m^2 or Pa   2 marks

Award two marks for the correct answer with unit, otherwise one mark.

> **Examiner's tip**
>
> 1 pascal (Pa) is the same as a N/m^2. Take care with units when doing pressure calculations. If the area is given in cm^2 then the correct unit is the N/cm^2.

TOTAL 5 MARKS

15a   Candle flame, the Sun and television screen   1 mark
  b   Light from the lamps is reflected off the actors and the stage   1 mark
       To all parts of the audience.   1 mark

> **Examiner's tip**
>
> Most objects that reflect light scatter it, so they reflect it in all directions. Only mirrors and other polished surfaces reflect the light in one particular direction.

  c   Green, red and yellow   1 mark

> **Examiner's tip**
>
> Yellow is a secondary colour; yellow light can be made by mixing red light and green light, so yellow filters and yellow objects subtract blue light from the light that reaches them.

  d   Black   1 mark

> **Examiner's tip**
>
> The actor's costume only reflects blue, and the yellow light does not contain any blue, so there is nothing for the costume to reflect.

TOTAL 5 MARKS

16a   Your Sun should be drawn lower than the Sun in spring.   1 mark
  b   The Earth's tilt and the Earth's movement around the Sun.   1 mark

Test A Answers

> **Examiner's tip**
>
> If the Earth wasn't tilted on its axis, the Sun's position in the sky would be the same, whatever the season.

   c   *Two reasons from:*
      Venus is closer to the Sun than Uranus.
      Venus reflects more light than Uranus does.
      Venus is closer to the Earth than Uranus.   *2 marks*

TOTAL 4 MARKS

17 a Biomass and wind   *1 mark*
    b More wood can be grown to replace any that is used.   *1 mark*

> **Examiner's tip**
>
> Whether a fuel is considered to be renewable depends on the time it takes to form. The time for wood to grow is very short when compared to the time it took for coal and oil to form.

TOTAL 2 MARKS

18 a Heat and movement (or kinetic)   *1 mark*
    b 96 J of heat   *1 mark*

> **Examiner's tip**
>
> This question is testing if you know that energy is conserved; none is ever used up.

TOTAL 2 MARKS

TEST TOTAL 91 MARKS

TEST B Pages 25–48

1 a Caterpillars   *1 mark*
   b Only plants are able to trap the energy from the Sun.   *1 mark*

> **Examiner's tip**
>
> The importance of photosynthesis to trap the energy from the Sun cannot be over-emphasised.

   c   The direction of energy flow through the food chain.   *1 mark*
   d (i) The great tit is a predator as it feeds on caterpillars.   *1 mark*
     (ii) The owl eats great tits and so great tits are the prey of owls.   *1 mark*
   e   Grass snake   *1 mark*

Test B Answers

> **Examiner's tip**
>
> Primary consumers eat plants, secondary consumers eat primary consumers, tertiary consumers eat secondary consumers.
>
> cabbage leaves ⟶ aphids ⟶ beetles ⟶ grass snake
>
> or
>
> cabbage leaves ⟶ aphids ⟶ frog ⟶ grass snake

f Grass snakes eat mice, frogs and beetles. *1 mark*
A shortage of beetles will have less effect on the grass snakes; *1 mark*
great tits do not have alternative food sources.

TOTAL 8 MARKS

2 Heart
Lung
Liver
Stomach *4 marks*

TOTAL 4 MARKS

3a A hinge joint *1 mark*

> **Examiner's tip**
>
> Hinge joints such as the elbow and the knee allow movement in one dimension only; all-round movement is allowed by ball and socket joints such as the shoulder.

b The biceps contract to pull on the forearm. *1 mark*

> **Examiner's tip**
>
> Like a piece of string, muscles can only pull; they cannot push.

c The biceps relax and the triceps contract. *1 mark*

> **Examiner's tip**
>
> The biceps and triceps are called an antagonistic pair of muscles because they act in opposite directions.

TOTAL 3 MARKS

4a B A D C *3 marks*
Award 1 mark if B is before A, 1 mark if A is before D and 1 mark if D is before C.

b The production of new cells by mitosis is faster in the sideshoot than in older stems. *1 mark*

Test B Answers

c Removing leaves reduces loss of water from the shoot.   *1 mark*
Removing all leaves stops photosynthesis.   *1 mark*

           TOTAL 6 MARKS

5a (i) To transport water from the roots to the leaves.   *1 mark*
   (ii) The cell is hollow so water can move through it.   *1 mark*
b (i) carbon dioxide + water + energy ⟶ sugar + oxygen   *2 marks*

Examiner's tip

One mark is given for the answer before the arrow and one for the answer after the arrow.

   (ii) Photosynthesis does not take place in the white portions of the leaves, only the green.   *1 mark*
c (i) Less sunny day *or* less water *or* too hot *or* too cold   *1 mark*
   (ii)

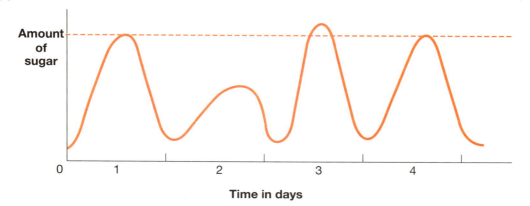

           1 mark
d (i) Respiration   *1 mark*
   (ii) Oxygen   *1 mark*

Examiner's tip

The understanding of the processes of photosynthesis and respiration is important. The equation for respiration is:

sugar + oxygen ⟶ carbon dioxide + water

N.B. This is the reverse of the equation for photosynthesis.

           TOTAL 9 MARKS

6a (i) The particles are held together by strong forces.   *1 mark*
   (ii) The ice lolly melts.   *1 mark*
   (iii) The particles gain enough energy to move around.   *1 mark*

Test B Answers

b   A gas is squashy, i.e. its volume changes as pressure increases.   *1 mark*
c   Expands on heating   *1 mark*

> **Examiner's tip**
>
> It is important to know how particles are arranged in solids, liquids and gases and the differences in the motion of particles in the three states. This should enable you to explain some of the properties of solids, liquids and gases.

d   When pressure is applied to the pedal, it is transferred to the gas but the gas volume decreases. The pressure is not transferred to the brake pad.   *1 mark*

TOTAL 6 MARKS

7 a   Distillation   *1 mark*
b   Filtration   *1 mark*
c   Fractional distillation   *1 mark*

> **Examiner's tip**
>
> Methods of separation are frequently tested. Distillation is used to separate a liquid from a dissolved solid. Fractional distillation is used to separate mixtures of liquids.

TOTAL 3 MARKS

8 a   Magnesium
       Zinc
       Iron
       Copper   *2 marks*

> **Examiner's tip**
>
> You are not expected to remember the order of reactivity of these metals but to work it out from the information given. One mark would be awarded for a slight error, e.g. zinc, magnesium, iron, copper.

b   Magnesium + hydrochloric acid ⟶ magnesium chloride + hydrogen   *2 marks*

> **Examiner's tip**
>
> A word equation is a summary of the reaction taking place, with the reacting substances (reactants) on the left-hand side and the products on the right-hand side. You will be expected to write word equations in these papers.

TOTAL 4 MARKS

Test B Answers

9a Zinc sulphide *1 mark*

Examiner's tip

Zinc sulphide is the name of the compound formed when zinc and sulphur combine. Note that the name ends in -ide, showing two elements are present, and the metal is written first. Zinc sulphate is a compound containing zinc and sulphur that also contains oxygen.

b (i) D *1 mark*
(ii) B *1 mark*
(iii) A *1 mark*

TOTAL 4 MARKS

10a The movement of particles is random (i.e. according to no pattern). *1 mark*
The particles are able to move past each other. *1 mark*

Examiner's tip

The arrangement and movement of particles in solids, liquids and gases are frequently tested. It is important to emphasise that the liquid state is intermediate between solid and gas.

b (i) Evaporation *1 mark*
(ii) The particles escape from the liquid. *1 mark*
These particles mix with the air. *1 mark*

Examiner's tip

It is important to understand the process of evaporation.

(iii) The particles which escape from the liquid are ones with high kinetic energy. *1 mark*
This means the liquid remaining is cooler and the hand feels colder. *1 mark*
c This is to reduce the evaporation of water from the reservoir. *1 mark*

TOTAL 8 MARKS

11a Magnesium
Lead
Copper
Silver
Award one mark if one metal is out of place. *2 marks*

Examiner's tip

You are not expected to remember the order of reactivity of these metals but to work it out from the information given.

Test B Answers

b	The blue colour of the solution fades.	1 mark
	Brown solid copper is formed.	1 mark

> **Examiner's tip**
>
> This question is about the changes you would see when lead is added to copper nitrate solution. Often students ignore this and just name the products.

c	Zinc + copper sulphate ⟶ zinc sulphate + copper	2 marks

TOTAL 6 MARKS

12a	B	1 mark
b	D	1 mark

> **Examiner's tip**
>
> Opposite magnetic poles attract each other; similar poles repel.

c	Your arrow should point directly away from the steel bar.	1 mark

> **Examiner's tip**
>
> This question is testing whether you know that the arrows on magnetic field lines show the direction of the force on the north-seeking pole of another magnet.

TOTAL 3 MARKS

13a	The magnetic field of the coil magnetises the iron.	1 mark
	The iron has a strong magnetic field.	1 mark
b	Wind more turns of wire or increase the current in the coil or the voltage of the battery.	1 mark

> **Examiner's tip**
>
> It is important to refer to the magnetic field when you explain effects due to electromagnetism.

TOTAL 3 MARKS

14a	A and C	1 mark
b	B	1 mark

> **Examiner's tip**
>
> The ratio of cells to lamps is the same in circuits **A** and **C**, but higher in **B**, causing a greater current.

TOTAL 2 MARKS

Test B Answers

15a Your arrow should point down. *1 mark*
It should be labelled either 'the pull of the Earth on the boat' or 'weight'. *1 mark*

Examiner's tip

Avoid using the term 'gravity'. It can be confusing because the word is often used to mean two different things: the gravitational field of the Earth and the effect of that field in pulling things towards the Earth.

b They are equal. *1 mark*

Examiner's tip

The forces acting on an object that is not moving must always be balanced; so a force in one direction is balanced by an equal-sized force acting in the opposite direction.

c It increases. *1 mark*

Examiner's tip

The boat is heavier when a person gets in, so the upward force must increase to keep the forces in balance.

TOTAL 4 MARKS

16a The speed is increasing. *1 mark*
The driving force is bigger than the resistive force. *1 mark*
b The yacht slows down. *1 mark*
The force on it is in the opposite direction to its motion. *1 mark*
Allow the last mark if you answered that the resistive force is the only force acting.

TOTAL 4 MARKS

17a D *1 mark*
b (i) E *1 mark*
(ii) Same size, upright, virtual *2 marks*
Allow one mark if two are correct.
c Refraction *1 mark*

TOTAL 5 MARKS

18a It moves further. *1 mark*
b It is higher pitched. *1 mark*

Test B Answers

Examiner's tip
This question is testing whether you know that the pitch of a note depends on the frequency and the loudness depends on the amplitude of the vibration.

TOTAL 2 MARKS

19 a Your line should be an arc across the sky, ending in the bottom right-hand corner of the diagram. *1 mark*
b The Earth spins on its own axis. *1 mark*

Examiner's tip
The apparent daily movement of the Sun in the sky is caused by the Earth's rotation on its axis.

TOTAL 2 MARKS

20 a The telephone conversations are transmitted to the satellite as radio waves. *1 mark*
The satellite amplifies them and transmits them back to Earth. *1 mark*
b The Earth pulls the satellite *1 mark*
With a gravitational force. *1 mark*

Examiner's tip
There is only one force on the satellite; the Earth's gravitational pull keeps it in orbit around the Earth.

TOTAL 4 MARKS

21 a The water has (gravitational) potential energy. *1 mark*
This is transferred to kinetic energy as it falls, which is used to generate electricity. *1 mark*
b *Allow one mark each for two of the following points:* *2 marks*
Not all of the potential energy of the water is transferred to kinetic energy.
The water does not lose all its kinetic energy when it passes through the generators; it is still moving when it leaves them.
Not all of the kinetic energy that the water loses when it passes through the generator is transferred to electricity.

Examiner's tip
You should appreciate that in an energy transfer process involving movement, some heating always occurs, causing some of the energy to be spread out in the surroundings.

c It allows surplus energy to be stored at night and used during the day. *1 mark*
Fewer power stations need to be built to cope with peak demand. *1 mark*

TOTAL 6 MARKS
TEST TOTAL 96 MARKS

Determining your level

FINDING YOUR LEVEL IN TESTS A AND B
When you have completed and marked a test, enter the total number of marks you scored for each question on the Marking Grid overleaf. Then add them up. Using the total for each test, look at the charts below to determine your level for each test.

Test A

Level 3 or below	Level 4	Level 5	Level 6	Level 7 or above
up to 12	13–31	32–49	50–69	70+

Test B

Level 3 or below	Level 4	Level 5	Level 6	Level 7 or above
up to 12	13–33	34–51	52–71	72+

FINDING YOUR OVERALL LEVEL IN SCIENCE
After you have worked out separate levels for Tests A and B, add up your total marks for the two tests. Use this total and the chart below to determine your overall level in Science. The chart also shows you how your level in these tests compares with the target level for your age group.

Total for Tests A and B

Level 3 or below	Level 4	Level 5	Level 6	Level 7 or above
up to 24	25–64	65–100	101–140	141+
Working towards target level for age group		Working at target level for age group		Working beyond target level

Marking Grid

TEST A Pages 1–24

Question	Marks available	Marks scored	Question	Marks available	Marks scored
1	15		10	2	
2	8		11	4	
3	3		12	4	
4	10		13	4	
5	3		14	5	
6	5		15	5	
7	2		16	4	
8	6		17	2	
9	7		18	2	
			Total	91	

TEST B Pages 25–48

Question	Marks available	Marks scored	Question	Marks available	Marks scored
1	8		12	3	
2	4		13	3	
3	3		14	2	
4	6		15	4	
5	9		16	4	
6	6		17	5	
7	3		18	2	
8	4		19	2	
9	4		20	4	
10	8		21	6	
11	6		Total	96	